MW01632503

Michael C.

experiencing **worship**

For everyone who desires a closer and more intimate relationship with the Heavenly Father, who created us and desires to have fellowship with us. May we all grow to be the worshipers that God would have us be. May our lives be full of praise and thanksgiving. To God be the glory forever and ever! Amen.

experiencing **worship**

INTRODUCTION

It appears that the age-old struggle in the area of worship in our churches will continue for some time. We long to lead our churches into deeper worship, but we often don't know how. This study will attempt to help us in our efforts to better understand biblical worship, the place it has in today's church, how it can transform our own walk with God, and how we can help lead others into true worship.

If you have read or gone through the study entitled *Experiencing God*, you know that there is more to the Christian life than just going to church on Sundays. You know that there is more than just praying once in a while when you need something from the Lord. Henry Blackaby, in his insightful study, gives us seven practical steps that help us experience God in the way that He intended us to know Him. This is a great study for the Christian who truly desires to be all that God created him to be. If you desire to deepen your walk with the Lord and experience Him and all that He has for your life, I encourage you to take the time to go through *Experiencing God.*

Similarly, in this study, I hope to offer you some practical ways that you can experience worship. While worship is only a part of our relationship with Christ, it actually becomes the medium through which all other areas of our Christian lives line up. Without worship, our prayer time becomes one sided. We become receivers and not givers, always asking for something instead of offering.

True worship, on the other hand, stems from a more mature and intimate relationship with the Lord. It is the time when we *give* to the Lord through our singing, praising, and declaring His holiness. It is more than a life of prayer and Bible study. It is more than a quiet time together with the Lord. Worship is what comes out of a realization of who God is and what He means to us *personally.* When we understand God in a genuine, personal way, we naturally want to give praise to the Lord for who He is in our lives. Becoming a *true* worshiper is stepping fully into who God designed us to be.

Let me state up front that this study does not present itself to be a complete guide to worship. It does not attempt to explain in full all there is to know about worship. It is merely an introduction to praise and worship and is meant to help people *begin* to understand true biblical worship and begin to become true worshipers.

To that end, *Experiencing Worship* offers a brief study of worship to be done in a small-group setting. This study can be used as a tool for the worship leaders and worship teams in your church as they grow in their leadership roles. It can be used in choir rehearsals to help the choir members better understand their roles in leading worship. It is designed to teach all of the leaders in music to become more than just singers or players. May they become the true worshipers that God would have them be.

In addition to the musicians in your church, this study could even be used in your family, because it is really written for *any* Christian who desires to better understand worship. My heart's desire is for all Christians to understand true biblical worship and that they, in turn, will teach others how to experience God in this way.

Just as many people miss out on all that God would have for them in this life, so too, many Christians miss out on the most important thing we can do — worship Him. I once read that the only thing Christians do on earth that we will still do in heaven is worship. If that is true, we should understand what we are doing now, because we will spend an eternity doing it. I do not want to waste my life merely *pretending* to worship when God's desire is for us to worship Him in spirit and truth *now.* He never said, "Wait until you get to heaven; then I will show you how to worship." He desires it each day of our lives, from the moment we accept Jesus as our Savior and Lord until the day we die. In fact, you will discover that God *requires* and even *commands* those who call Jesus "Savior" to worship Him.

During this study, you will be involved in six weeks of studying the Bible, practicing various expressions of worship, and reading through a daily devotional. Each week, you will discover something new about worship. When you get together with your group, you will share with each other what you have experienced and your findings in the scriptures. You will begin a new life of worship together as you put into practice true biblical worship.

This study is outlined as follows:

WEEK 1 - WHY DO WE WORSHIP?

WEEK 2 - WHAT IS WORSHIP?

WEEK 3 - WHAT IS PRAISE?

WEEK 4 - CORPORATE AND PERSONAL WORSHIP

WEEK 5 - A TRUE WORSHIPER

I hope that you will pursue a life of true worship that is pleasing and honoring to the Lord. I pray as you seek out what God has for you in *Experiencing Worship* that you will allow the Holy Spirit to speak to you personally. My desire is that through prayer, studying the scriptures, and trying new worship ideas, you will come away with a new and fresh heart for worship. God wants to draw you closer to Himself. He loves you, He has saved you, and He wants you to have the fullest life possible – *in Him.*

You will see through this study that worship is more than just coming to church on Sunday to sing a few songs and listen to a sermon. You can worship the Lord every day in true biblical worship. As I share bits and pieces of my journey as a worshiper, I pray that my limited knowledge and understanding will help you begin this exciting journey of expressing your heart to our Creator and Lord.

I have also included the *Experiencing Worship Devotional* in this new edition of the study. It is designed for you to read each day between your weekly group sessions. There are five days of devotions each week to help deepen your understanding and experience of worship. I pray that they will help and bless you in your personal journey.

experiencing **worship**

WEEK 1

WHY DO WE WORSHIP?

experiencing **worship**

What would you like to gain from this study?

I encourage you to begin each session with prayer asking the Father to reveal what He desires from you in regard to worship and your relationship to Him. Because prayer is an essential part of worship, spend at least 5-10 minutes in prayer before you continue.

Take a few minutes to answer the questions below. Plan to share your answers with your group. When the study is finished, you will be asked to answer these questions again and to compare your responses.

In your own words, give your definition of worship.

"Let everything that hath breath praise the Lord." Psalm 150:6 (KJV)

What is the place of worship in a Christian's life as you understand it?

why do we worship?

What is the place of worship in your life now?

____

____

____

____

"But the hour is coming, and now is, when the true worshipers will worship the Father in spirit and truth; for the Father is seeking such to worship Him." John 4:23 (NKJV)

According to this verse, what kind of worship does the Father want from us?

____

____

____

____

experiencing **worship**

What does that look like in our world today?

____

____

____

Do you feel you are a true worshiper? (Circle one.)

Yes No Sometimes Not Sure

It is very important to understand that the Father is not seeking worship itself, but worshipers. Worship fosters a dynamic relationship between the Father and us, His children. In John 4:23, the word "seeking" is *zeteo* in the Greek. It carries the same tone as "require" or "demand." What does this mean? Our Father is *requiring* or *demanding* us to worship Him in spirit and truth.

WHY DO WE WORSHIP?

The need or desire to worship is born in every person. It is not something that is taught or developed. It is created within us to do. Think of any culture in the world that you may be familiar with. No explorer has ever found a tribe or culture that did not worship. Every culture worships something or someone. Some worship false gods or idols, while others worship money or even self. Because we are born with a desire and instinct to worship, the question is not "Do we worship?" but "*What or whom* do we worship?"

If we learn to worship God and not our selfish interests, in God's perfect generosity and grace, our lives will be fuller and richer. Graham Kendrick was right when he said, "*Worship is first and foremost for His benefit, not ours, though it is marvelous to discover that in giving Him pleasure, we ourselves enter into what can become our richest and most wholesome experience in life.*"[1]

In fact, worship is not just born in us, it is what we were made for. As Don McMinn expresses it, *"Our entire being is fashioned as an instrument of praise. Just as a master violin maker designs an instrument to produce maximum aesthetic results, so God tailor-made our bodies, souls and spirits to work together in consonance to produce pleasing expressions of praise and worship. When we use body language to express praise, that which is internal becomes visible."* [2]

What would you say if I told you that worship is the *most important thing* a Christian can do? Many of you might object. You might respond that evangelism is the most important thing we do as Christians. We are told to "go and tell." Consider this debate by answering a few questions.

Why do you feel we were created?

____

____

____

> *"Then God spoke all these words, saying, 'I am the LORD your God, who brought you out of the land of Egypt, out of the house of slavery. You shall have no other gods before Me.'"* Exodus 20:1-3 (NASB)

According to the passage above, what was the first commandment given to Moses?

____

____

____

____

Did you know that we are *called* to worship? Worship is not optional for the children of God. It's not something that we can decide to do if we feel like it. Worship is the first commandment that God gave to Moses.

The Lord goes on to say in the next verses, *"You shall not make for yourself an idol, or any likeness of what is in heaven above or on the earth beneath or in the water under the earth. You shall not worship them or serve them; for I, the Lord your God, am a jealous God... ."* Exodus 20:4-5 (NASB)

God's first and second commandments dealt with worshiping Him and Him alone.

Exodus 34:14 (NASB) says, *"...for you shall not worship any other god, for the Lord, whose name is Jealous, is a jealous God...."*

Because we were created to worship to have fellowship with God, nothing else we do in life will fill that void. Until our relationship with God and our worship life is meeting the core need in our lives, we will not be able to truly find happiness or fulfillment in anything else.

Have you ever set out to fulfill a goal in your life? Did you find that after you met the goal that you still felt empty? Maybe you decided that reaching a certain financial level would help to make your life better. Then when you reached it, nothing really changed. You just found more debt and frustration. In many cases, the desire to continue to earn more becomes lord. It rules your life.

We see this kind of idolatry even in marriages, which may help us see why so many fail. Some of us expect from a mate what we can only find in God. Yet the truth is we cannot have a truly full and rich marriage without first having a full and rich relationship with God.

So many times in looking for a mate, we look for someone who will fill that emptiness we all have inside. When we find someone, our expectations and demands are far too high. We are asking that person to fill the void that only God can through a personal relationship with Him. When we demand this from other people, we doom them to failure. They can never meet the needs that God is designed to meet.

If we find what we need in God, we will not need to look for it in others or in things. The Lord desires that we develop a close relationship with Him. When this is first, your marriage will naturally be closer and more intimate. Develop a relationship with God that meets the core need of your life first, and your relationships will be much more fulfilling. They will become the icing on the cake – not the only ingredients in it.

Even as a Christian though, I sometimes find myself thinking I need something more in life. I don't mean to be worldly, but sometimes I am. I get sidetracked from Him, distracted, drawn to things that look fulfilling or exciting for the moment. I end up feeling frustrated and deceived and even emptier than ever. That is exactly why God instructs us to worship Him only. He wants only the best for us, and He knows that everything else we worship will leave us empty.

What does Matthew 6:33 say?

____

____

____

What does Romans 12:1 tell us?

____

____

____

If worship is the most important thing we can do as Christians then what about Jesus' last command to us to "go and tell"? Like many of you, I was always under the impression that our main purpose in life was to share Jesus with others. For years, I believed that the Great Commission was the main focus of every devoted Christian.

But lately God has been teaching me that first and foremost worship and a close relationship with Him is our calling. You see, if we are truly people of worship – not just in the church on Sunday – but if we are truly people who love God and worship Him with our total being, we will naturally draw people to Christ through our lives of worship.

Maybe you have met people like this. They seem connected to God. They speak His words naturally. They are kind, compassionate, and set apart. They make you want to be around them to learn what they know. This is how worship becomes the tool to fulfill the Great Commission. When the world sees genuine worshipers, they will be drawn to them, not because of us or what we do, but because of God's presence in us.

So, yes, we must go and tell others of Christ, but first of all, we must worship. When we worship God and die to ourselves, it is then that He takes what we give and turns it into something greater than we can ever create ourselves. It is then that people will come to Christ and will draw others into becoming true worshipers.

SAVED TO WORSHIP

Have you ever thought about why God sent His Son to die on the cross for you? I asked you earlier to state why you felt you were created. Was it to keep you from hell? Was it so your life would be easier? Why did God choose to send His only Son to die on a cross for you?

John 3:16 (NASB) states, *"For God so loved the world that He gave His only begotten Son, that whoever believes in Him should not perish, but have eternal life."*

I believe that *love* was what motivated God to send His Son. He loves us that much. He desires for us to spend eternity with Him. And what do you think we will do in heaven for eternity?

Read Revelation 4:8-11. What does John say about what he saw in heaven?

____

____

____

____

God saves us so that we might spend eternity with Him, so that we might be the worshipers that He seeks in John 4:23 (NKJV): "*But an hour is coming, and now is, when the* ***true worshipers*** *shall worship the Father in spirit and truth, for such the Father seeks to be His worshipers.*"

Who is a true worshiper? First, this verse implies that a true worshiper is a Christian, one who has the spirit of God and follows His truth. In fact, every Christian should be a worshiper. Let's look a bit further in scripture.

Read Acts 18:13. What did the Corinthian leaders claim that Paul was trying to persuade the people to do?

____

____

____

Paul was a missionary traveling around spreading the good news of Christ so that people could become saved. When they became saved, they naturally became worshipers. Worship was the visible outflow of an internal conversion. Is it for us today?

When I first realized the truth of Jesus and the cross, I discovered that God loved me and desired for me to give my life to Him. I wept, fell on my knees, praised Him, and worshiped Him. It was a natural response to what Christ had done for me. This response was not unique to my situation. Similar responses are revealed a number of times in the scriptures. Let's look at a few verses. List the different responses of worship:

Matthew 2: 11 ____________________________

Matthew 8:1-2 ____________________________

Matthew 9:18 ____________________________

Matthew 14:33 ____________________________

Matthew 28:9 ____________________________

God does not save us for our sakes, but for His. We are saved in order to worship Him. Because of our great redemption, we are to worship.

As Christians, the question we should be asking is not "Should we worship?" or "Whom do we worship?" but "*How* do we worship?" What does it mean to worship "in *spirit and truth*?" Next week we will look at worship that is acceptable to the Lord and worship that is unacceptable.

The following exercises are designed to help you begin a life of worship. They are not to manipulate you into worship but to help you in your journey toward a more worship-filled life.

Exercise for Week 1 - Every time the spirit prompts you to remember, voice externally: "Praise the Lord. I praise you, God, for who You are."

That's all. Each time you think about it, voice this simple praise to the Lord. Do this every day this week.

Write down what you experienced after the first week. Plan to share this with those in your group.

I have included the *Experiencing Worship Devotional* for you in this study to read each day of the week between sessions. I hope it adds to your growth as a worshiper.

Remember: ***Worship is not about the style of music but about the heart. Music is only a tool to better help us worship the Lord. To label worship with music is to limit the expression.***

DAILY DEVOTIONS

WEEK 1

experiencing **worship**

DAY 1

"*After coming into the house they saw the Child with Mary His mother, and they fell to the ground and worshiped Him. Then, opening their treasures, they presented to Him gifts of gold, frankincense, and myrrh.*" Matthew 2:11 (NASB)

If there is one form of worship missing in our churches today, it's the willingness to bow before the Lord. I'm not talking about the "bowing of our hearts" or a "spirit" of bowing; I'm talking about literally bowing on our knees. Why is it that we have such a difficult time doing this?

Throughout the Bible, there are many instances in which bowing precedes the word "worship." In fact, in most references to worship, *bowing* is used as a response.

As you begin your day, spend some time in worship before the Lord. Try kneeling before Him. This is a hard thing to do for many of us, yet if He were an earthly king, it would be natural, even demanded in some cultures. So, why not for the spiritual King?

God is the King of ALL kings and our actions should reflect His Lordship. He is worthy of our humility, and it is good for our growth as worshipers to physically humble ourselves to Him. If the goal of a worshiper is to die to self, we should not be ashamed to bow before the Lord. We will grow as worshipers as we strive to be obedient to His word in this area of worshiping Him.

DAY 2

"*...for we are the true circumcision, who worship in the Spirit of God and glory in Christ Jesus and put no confidence in the flesh, ...*" Philippians 3:3 (NASB)

Have you ever been to a worship service where it seemed there was little evidence of God's Spirit? Have you ever walked into your church and sat through the service thinking, "There has to be more than this?"

I have attended many "worship services" that appeared to be no more than just a "service." They seemed to lack a genuine movement of the Holy Spirit. For the most part, they were good services with good music and a decent lesson, but that isn't a *worship service.* Is that kind of service wrong? Maybe not, but let's call it what it is.

Philippians 3:3 says that true worship is done on a spiritual level, not on a fleshly level. If we are not worshiping in the spirit, with God's Spirit, our worship is in the flesh and will not be true worship. A worship service should be a time when we worship the Lord with our whole beings in the Spirit.

How would you rate your worship?

DAY 3

"Jesus said, 'Let the little children come to me, and do not hinder them, for the kingdom of heaven belongs to such as these." Matthew 19:14 (NIV)

One of my favorite times of spontaneous worship may seem kind of strange. It is not singing in corporate worship. It's not being alone with God in my private times, although each of these times is special. My favorite times are watching my children play. This might seem like an odd example of worship, but as they play or even just sit in their unique ways, they cause me to worship the Lord. I find myself thanking God for these amazing gifts He gave us, praising Him for these miracles. How can this be worship?

As I look at my children, I see the second greatest gift God has ever given me. After salvation, nothing compares to the gift of life. I watch them and am amazed at how God gives life through His creation. I am deeply moved that He would entrust these little ones to me. These times are truly emotional experiences of expressing love to the Father for what He has given me.

As you look at your children – or the children that God has placed in your life – remember that they are more than just kids; they are incredible creations from God. Be forever grateful that He allowed you to be blessed with them as part of your life.

DAY 4

"Worship the LORD with gladness; come before him with joyful songs." Psalm 100:2 (NIV)

It has always baffled me to watch certain "Christians" worship. Although we are all created different, although we are all unique in God's eyes, shouldn't we all be glad that God saved us and loves us? You would think so.

And yet there are many who come to church week after week looking like they'd rather be at the dentist. We stand to sing praise to the Lord and they look as though they are irritated to have to stand for a few minutes. They sing, "I've got the joy, joy, joy," when really they've got the blues, blues, blues.

When you really stop and think about the gift God has given us, you can't help but be glad. If you are not, then you don't understand the price that was paid, the gift that was given.

Sit down with the Father today and ask Him to open your eyes to the gift and its value. Thank Jesus for dying for you. It was a high price that should not be taken lightly. Be joyful and glad that HE chose to give it to you freely.

experiencing **worship**

DAY 5

"Enter his gates with thanksgiving and his courts with praise; give thanks to him and praise his name." Psalm 100:4 (NIV)

Have you ever given a costly gift to someone who never thanked you or just didn't seem as appreciative of it as you thought they should be? I wonder if God ever feels that way about us. What does He think when He gives us salvation, the greatest gift anyone could give, and yet we treat it as though it were a trinket?

Being grateful is a rare trait these days. In our society, we have so much and receive so much that we become expectant of more. We have lost the true ability to be grateful. "I work hard for what I get," we boast. "No one has helped me get where I am." We fail to remember that all good things come from the Father, most importantly, our salvation.

Worship is about giving back, and yet we have turned it into a time of expecting to get, trying to figure out what *God* can do for *us*, rather than what *we* can do for *God*. May we pause each day to give thanks to the Lord for giving us life through His Son. May we praise Him corporately as we gather together. May we give to Him in our worship. He is worthy and deserving of our thanks.

WEEK 2

WHAT IS WORSHIP?

experiencing **worship**

We have now looked at *why* we should worship and *whom* we should worship. The next question to consider is, "*How* should we worship?" What does it mean to worship in "spirit and truth?" What are acceptable expressions of "spiritual" worship? When is our worship unacceptable to God?

Worship can be defined as recognizing and proclaiming the worth, value, majesty, honor, and glory of God and giving homage, respect, reverence and praise to God. I also like the way Lamar Boschman states it in *A Heart for Worship*: *"Worship is the adoration, veneration, exaltation and magnification of God. When we praise, esteem, love, admire and celebrate God, we are worshipping Him. Worship is totally concerned with the worthiness of God and not the worthiness of the worshipper."*[3]

Genesis 18:2 uses the Hebrew word for worship, which is *shahah*. What is it that Abraham does that is *shahah* or worship?

____

Worship is something that we do. It comes from an acceptable inward attitude expressed *outwardly*, such as Abraham's bowing down. Worship is purely and solely for the Lord and should be a natural outflow of an inward attitude of our pure affection.

Where does worship start?

____

Can someone who doesn't know Christ as Savior truly worship God?

____

The answer to that question is obvious to those of us who know Christ as Savior. It is impossible to sincerely worship God if you don't sincerely love Him. If you do not yet know Him, take the time to invite Him into your heart today. Ask God to forgive you of your sins and become Lord of your life. Then you can begin a life of worship.

Worship begins as we understand who Christ is and what He means to us, how He saved us from death and hell, and how He gives us joy and abundant life here on earth. As we grow to know Him better through a personal relationship and through our prayer life and Bible study, we begin to develop a deeper part of that relationship – worship. This is the part where it becomes difficult at times to express how we feel because of the depth of our love.

When a man and wife get married, it is obvious that they love each other. As the relationship grows, it becomes more intimate and meaningful. It becomes more difficult to say in words what they feel for each other because all the words have been used up. Saying "I love you" is just not enough anymore. Likewise, in our expression to God of what He means to us, we must continually search for new words and ways to express to Him our deep devotion and love for Him. As a husband acknowledges the worth of his wife through loving her and showing that love in words and actions, so do we acknowledge God's worth through loving Him and expressing that love by continually pursuing a deeper and deeper relationship.

UNACCEPTABLE WORSHIP

It is crucial to understand that we do not worship merely the way we want. We cannot do anything we want and call it worship. Our worship must be biblical and acceptable to the Lord. Let's look at some instances in the Bible where people worshiped in their own way.

experiencing **worship**

Read Exodus 32:1-10 and explain what happened to the people of Israel.

____

____

____

____

It is important to note that these people *thought* they were still worshiping God. Their folly occurred when they made Him into an image, the golden calf. We cannot reduce God to an image or thing.

What was the result of their worshiping this image of God?
Exodus 32:25-28

____

____

Read Leviticus 10:1-3. Explain what happened.

____

____

What appeared to have happened there was that Nahab and Abihu presented an offering to the Lord that was not according to God's requirements. It was their offering, concocted by themselves and not God.

What was the result of their own self-styled worship? What happened to them?

____

____

Read Isaiah 2:6-10. Explain what happened to these people as a result of their straying from God's plan for worship.

____

____

____

Read Mark 7:6-9 and explain.

____

____

____

The Pharisees tended to do many things that were outwardly correct in their worship, yet their hearts were cold and their attitude was not acceptable to God. Having the right attitude is crucial in acceptable worship.

experiencing **worship**

ACCEPTABLE WORSHIP

What are acceptable ways to worship?

1. Psalm 24:3-6

____

2. Hebrews 12:28-29

____

3. Deut. 26:10

____

One of the most meaningful acts of worship recorded in the New Testament is in John 12:1-3.

What was the act of worship that was given to Jesus and by whom was it given?

____

____

____

In Acts 13:22, whom did God make king and what does He say about this person?

____

____

____

Read the following scriptures and give a brief summary of David's heart toward God and worship: Psalms 29:2, 95:6, 96:9, 99:5, 99:9, 132:7.

____

____

This is obviously a man who had a great heart of worship for the Lord. In verse after verse he gives praise and worship to God out of his love for Him.

Do you believe that with all that had happened to David – with the death of his child and the constant threat of his enemies – he was a man who *felt* like worshiping all the time?

____

____

Do you think that it was always easy for him to express praise to God amid the trials and difficult times?

____

____

Most of the time when we enter a worship service, what are we thinking? Do we think, "What can I receive from this service? I wonder if the worship leader picked any good songs this week? Will this leave me *feeling* that I have worshiped? I hope the sermon is funny this week." Is our focus on ourselves or on God?

When we enter a worship service, the question in our minds and hearts should always be, "What can I give today in worship – through my singing, listening, and participation – that will be pleasing to the Lord? How can I be obedient in worship and not seek self, but God?"

David did this very thing. Throughout the Psalms, David praised God and worshiped Him. His worship was an offering, based not on David's expectations or demands, but on his adoration of God. The result of his praise, however, was that God did bless him and protect him from his enemies. David praised God for His protection both before and after it had been given. In fact, David's worship was so consistent in good times and bad that he is referred to in the Bible as "a man after God's own heart." What a great honor!

Think about it like this. If you enter into any relationship with the attitude of "What can I get out of this relationship?" you will never experience real love. You will only desire to take and not give. When I think of the greatest act of love that anyone can do for another, I think of someone giving up his or her life for someone else. John 15:13 (NIV) says, "*Greater love has no one than this, that he lay down his life for his friends.*" The key here is *giving*. The same applies to worship. You cannot have a relationship with the Lord that is *true* without giving.

Read Gen. 22:5-18. How does this act relate to worship?

____

____

____

Read Verse 5 again. What did Abraham tell his servants he was going to do?

____

____

____

Abraham was obedient to the Lord in his willingness to sacrifice his son. The desire to please the Lord through giving his only son was the ultimate act of worship. He listened to the Lord and obeyed.

Read Psalm 27:6, 50:14, and 107:22 and Hebrews 13:15. What word is most common in each of these verses?

____

____

We sing, "*We bring a sacrifice of praise,*" but is it really a *sacrifice*? Some days I'm sure it is, and that's exactly what God desires of us in our worship. Sacrifice requires giving something up. In the Old Testament, God's people gave up the best of their flocks. God required their best. So it is with us in our worship today. God requires (or *zeteo*) our worship.

If you are like me, sometimes it takes a sacrifice of *self* to worship because we don't always feel like it. However, through our sacrifice, God honors and blesses our worship to the point that we end up receiving much more than we could ever give. When we enter our times of worship with the attitude of "How much can I give to the Lord today through my prayer, praise, singing, and listening?" then we will come away knowing that we have worshiped. Even in times when emotions are gone and our worship seems stale, keep in mind that worship is a choice, not a feeling. If we are faithful in our worship, God will be pleased.

Write down an experience in your life when you gave something without the thought of getting something in return. What was the result of that gesture?

____

____

experiencing **worship**

Just as with our tithing, we cannot out-give God in our worship and praise. He promises to respond when we are faithful to lift Him up.

We need to be careful when we worship that the expression is a result of what is real and true in us. As we read earlier in Psalm 24:3-6, our motives and hearts need to be in the right place. Many times we are caught mimicking other people in their worship or copying the worship leader. But worship must come from within you. It is a product of who you are in Christ and a result of your personal relationship with Him. Worship must be sincere.

Does worship end with the song service?

____

EXPRESSIONS OF WORSHIP

What are some of the expressions of worship listed in the following verses?

Psalm 100:2__________________________

2 Chronicles 6:19_____________________

Psalm 46:10__________________________

Lam. 3:41___________________________

Psalm 96:8___________________________

1 Tim. 4:13__________________________

1 Cor. 11:25-26_______________________

I love what Lamar Boschman says about sincerity in worship: "*When I worship, I would rather my heart be without words than my words be without heart.*"[4]

what is worship?

What does 1 Peter 2:5 say about how our worship should be?

____

____

____

____

Exercise for Week 2 - Continue to voice the simple offering of praise that you did in week one. This time add the phrase, "Father, I thank you for loving me and sending your Son to die for me. Thank you for all you have done in my life. I love you." This week, for your church worship service, come with the attitude of giving. Don't even think about what you want to get out of the service. Make your main focus giving to the Lord in singing, praying, listening, and reading scripture.

Write down what you experienced after the second week. Plan to share this with those in your group.

____

____

____

____

Go through your daily devotional.

DAILY DEVOTIONS

WEEK 2

experiencing **worship**

DAY 1

"All the nations you have made will come and worship before you, O Lord; they will bring glory to your name." Psalm 86:9 (NIV)

I can't wait to witness this event. All the nations of the world will gather to worship the Lord together. It will be *the* biggest worship event of all time. Can you imagine billions of people singing praises to the Lord together in unison? That will be a phenomenal thing to behold!

Why is it that we know this and yet we fail to worship from week to week? Why do we ignore this awesome experience that God desires for us? One day *all nations* will do it. One day *every* knee will bow and tongue confess that He is Lord. One day we will *all* stand before Him in awe as we worship the Almighty God. Shouldn't we begin preparing ourselves now? Isn't God worthy of our praise today, not only when we are in heaven?

Today is a good day to begin becoming the worshiper who God wants you to be. Start today with your praise and worship to the Father. It will change your life!

DAY 2

"Then I looked and heard the voice of many angels, numbering thousands upon thousands, and ten thousand times ten thousand. They encircled the throne and the living creatures and the elders. In a loud voice they sang: 'Worthy is the Lamb, who was slain, to receive power and wealth and wisdom and strength and honor and glory and praise!'" Revelation 5:11-12 (NIV)

Often we get so caught up in the rush and distractions of life that God takes a backseat. But do we ever stop and think of who God really is? In Revelation 4 and 5, John describes the throne room of God. He sees multitudes of angels, 24 elders laying their crowns at the feet of God, and four creatures. One is like a lion, one like an ox, one with the face of a man, and one like a flying eagle. Each has six wings and is covered with eyes. All of these phenomenal beings that seem so much bigger than John, and he watches them in amazement as they crumble before the Creator, humbling themselves and singing praises to Him. This is the same Creator who we toss into the backseat when our lives get busy ... the same Creator who we come before half-heartedly when we pray or when we sing in worship.

The next time you stop to pray or open your mouth to sing praises to God take a minute or two and place yourself in John's shoes. Picture yourself standing directly in front of the Creator himself, surrounded by these wondrous creatures, praising God together. Whenever we sing, whenever we pray, that's really where we are – in the throne room of our King and our Maker.

DAY 3

"Glory in his holy name; let the hearts of those who seek the LORD rejoice." 1 Chronicles 16:10 (NIV)

Are you still a seeker? Do you still seek to know God better? Have you grown weary in your efforts to spend time with the Lord? Has the flame and excitement that came with your salvation gone? Is your relationship with the Father stale and old? Keeping up a relationship with God takes time. In fact, every relationship takes time. We all make a choice – conscious or unconscious – of who will receive our time.

The verse above states, "Let the hearts of those who seek the Lord *rejoice*." What does it mean to rejoice? It means "feel happiness or joy, to express great joy, be ecstatic with joy." Let's face it. This is a hard thing to do, especially when we are not in a right relationship with God. We might try to fake it, but without the heart, we fall short of true praise and worship.

If we truly seek Him, our hearts will rejoice and be glad. Why? Because we see Him for who He is as Lord. We see more closely what He has done for us. When we fall in love with the Lord, rejoicing will fall from our lips without thought or effort. It will be the natural result of seeking Him and finding Him!

"Rejoice in the Lord always. I will say it again: Rejoice!"
Philippians 4:4 (NIV)

Now that I am seeking Him everyday, now that I've made the choice to know God better, how can I rejoice in Him always? Come on, *always*?! That's too much for anyone, right?

When we look again at the word *rejoice,* we have to accept its true meaning. Rejoicing is not for us; it's for God. He is worthy of our praise and celebration. When we celebrate our children's birthdays, it's not about us but them. We honor them with a cake, gifts, a party, or a birthday song, because we love them so much. Similarly, when we truly stop and think of what Jesus did for each of us and how much we love Him, we cannot help but be glad and rejoice in Him.

Keep in mind that the Bible never says we are to rejoice when we feel like it. We are to rejoice *always*! The author of this verse even goes as far as to repeat himself. Even when we don't want to, we need to be glad in the Lord. I once asked a friend of mine, "How are you so happy all the time?" He responded, "When I wake up in the morning, I have the opportunity to make a choice. Will I be happy or not? I choose to be happy!" The same thing holds true of our rejoicing, and when we make a *choice to rejoice,* God will honor it.

DAY 5

"All the earth bows down to you; they sing praise to you, they sing praise to your name." Psalm 66:4 (NIV)

Have you ever looked at tree branches blowing in the wind and wondered, "Are they praising God with their motions?" The limbs gently sway back and forth as if they had their hands raised in praise. Or listen to the wind itself – the noise it makes as it whistles through a valley. How about the oceans waves as they crash against the shore? If you step outside and close your eyes, you can hear many sounds made by nature. Could it be that these very sounds are constant praise to the Lord? It would be safe to say that the ocean never stops moving and the wind is always blowing ... somewhere. How awesome to think that everything God created praises Him all the time, forever and ever.

What should this say to us? We as humans have so much more to be grateful for than the trees do. God has given us the greatest gift of all –Jesus. May we become as the earth and praise Him in all we do. May our singing be a joyful sound. May our hearts worship Him constantly. May we become imitators of the earth as we offer our praise to the Lord.

NOTES

WEEK 3

WHAT IS PRAISE?

experiencing **worship**

In your own words give your definition of praise.

How does praise fit into your worship times?

Do you feel that praise is different from worship? Why?

Which is more important, praise or worship? Why?

what is praise?

If the highest duty of the angels is to give praise to God, then it would seem that it should be one of our highest priorities as well.

A few definitions given for praise in the dictionary are "to commend; to applaud; to express approval or admiration of; to extol in words or in song; to magnify; to glorify … ." Praise can be understood from the original meaning ***to be something we say or sing***. We do it all the time when we express to an employee how well he or she is doing or to our children when they do something great like getting a good report card. We can praise people directly to them or we can praise them by telling others about them.

Similarly, praise can be directed to God or directed to others about God. Either way, it is vocal in its expression. Praise is voicing how we feel about all that He has done for us. And yet God is worthy of our praise just for who He is.

What does Psalm 66:8 say about our praise?

____

____

Praise creates an atmosphere for the presence of the Lord. What happens when we offer up praise to the living Lord? Psalm 22:3

____

____

It is interesting to me that in the Old Testament people often named their children according to the children's personalities or character. God Himself was known as Jehovah-Raphah because He was, literally, the God who heals. In Genesis 22, God reveals Himself as Jehovah-Jireh because He would be the God who provides for His people. Leah kept with the Hebrew tradition when she named her fourth son Judah.

experiencing **worship**

Read Genesis 29:35. What does Judah mean?

____

Judah means praise. Is it a coincidence that God chose Judah as the tribe to which the Messiah was born or that the scriptures speak of the tribe of Judah more than any other? Let's look at a few verses to see how Judah or praise was used:

Psalm 114:2 _______________________________________

Psalm 76:1 _______________________________________

Psalm 108:8 _______________________________________

Now replace the word "Judah" with the word "praise." Psalm 114:2 (NIV) says that "*Judah* (literally, "praise") *became God's sanctuary.*" If praise is God's sanctuary, it is a good thing to give praise to the Lord (Psalm 92:1). If we want the Lord to dwell in our hearts and lives, praise must be present in us. He *inhabits* the praises of His people.

The reason so many churches lack the presence and power of God is because praise is lacking in them.

How many times have you gone to church and sat in the pew thinking, "I don't feel like singing today" or "I'm not in the mood to praise the Lord today"? Hey, I have! If crossing my arms and standing there looking at my watch is my expression of praise, it will never be acceptable to God. The Bible gives us clear direction on how we are to praise and worship Him.

Isaiah 43:21 (NASB) says, *"The people whom I formed for Myself will declare My praise."*

Does this scripture say that we "might" declare His praises or "if we feel like it" we will declare His praises? No. It states that we ***will*** declare His praises – that is why we were formed. It is not an option. We will praise Him now or we *will* praise Him later, but be sure that we will praise Him. And how much sweeter it is if we choose it freely now and praise Him often!

Look up Hebrews 13:15 (NASB) and fill in the missing word here: *"Through Him then, let us continually offer up a* ________________ *of praise to God, that is, the fruit of lips that give thanks to His name."*

When I think of sacrificing something, it usually involves me doing something that is very difficult or that I really don't want to do. In the same way, I don't believe that God desired to let His Son die for us on the cross. I believe that it was a great sacrifice for Him to do so.

We all do things out of sacrifice, don't we? We give up smoking so we can have better health. We sacrifice our sleep to feed the baby. We go without seconds on dessert so we can fit into our clothes. Whatever it is that we believe in, we will *sacrifice* for it. This is how praise should be. If we are honest with ourselves, we will admit that we don't always feel like giving praise to God. It will, at times, need to be a sacrifice of praise to God, doing it not because we want to all the time, but because He is worthy of it and we know that. Praise is not based upon our feelings but upon God's greatness, and – unlike our feelings – His greatness never changes.

When those of us who are parents give up things for our children, we do it because our children are worth it — or worthy of it — in our eyes and hearts. Sometimes we don't particularly feel like it, especially when they are not acting exactly as we would like them to act. The same and even more applies to God — for He is worthy of our praise even when our lives are not going exactly as we would like them to go.

I hope that there will be times, more often than not, when our praise to God will come from a joyful heart. It will be an expression of true joy as we lift Him up in our expressions of praise. This is what the Lord desires. Ask Him to develop in you a heart that joyfully gives Him praise, honor, and glory.

Read the following:

Psalm 9:2 ______________________________________

Psalm 33:1______________________________________

Psalm 43:4 ______________________________________

Why should we praise our Lord?

Psalm 150:1___________________________

Psalm 22:3 ___________________________

Acts 16:26 ___________________________

Psalm 48:1 ___________________________

1 Peter 2:9 ___________________________

1 Chron. 16:25 ________________________

Is it the responsibility of the worship pastor or pastor to lead us into praise of the Father? ______

Why? ____

____

____

When should I praise the Lord? There are many instances in scripture that exhort us to praise Him in the morning or at midnight. The verse I like best that gives insight on this is Psalm 34:1.

What does it say about when we should offer praise?

____

____

____

I feel that it is important to look at one other aspect of praise. If you are like me, giving praise to God is something that you do in church for the most part. Maybe you even do some praising when you're alone in your car or office. But one place where I fail to praise Him is in public around non-believers. Is that scriptural?

Read Psalm 40:3. What does it tell us about praise?

____

____

____

experiencing **worship**

Try Psalm 96:3

____

____

What an incredible thing—praise! God is honored by it, He desires it, it is good for us, and it draws people to Him.

What are some expressions of praise listed in the verses below?

Psalm 28:2, 63:4 ________________________

Psalm 47:1 ____________________________

Psalm 150:3-5 __________________________

2 Chron.29:26 __________________________

Psalm 95:6 _____________________________

Psalm 33:1-3 ___________________________

Psalm 149:3 ____________________________

Psalm 66:1_____________________________

How ever we view these different aspects of praise, we cannot deny that they are in the scriptures and that they were used as praise in public and private worship. When considering what praise is, we can recall the verse in Psalm 103:1.

What is key in this verse to remember about praise?

____

____

What is central to Mark 12:30?

____

____

It has been my experience that many churches do a fairly good job at giving praise to God. Most of the songs in our hymnals that are praise-oriented are based on the goodness of God and what He has done for us. Many even directly praise the Lord.

Can you think of three songs that your church uses to praise the Lord? List them below.

____

____

____

How do these songs help you to praise God?

____

____

____

Many churches and believers feel that they cannot give celebrative praise to the Lord during their public worship. They feel that visitors might think badly of them or that they may be a distraction or a stumbling block. Actually, quite the opposite is true. When we exalt the Lord in our corporate times of worship, if it is genuine and real, others will be drawn to the Lord. They will see something real within us that they have never experienced before. They will be drawn to the One who can save them from death and hell. Through our life of worship and praise, others will want to come to know Him and to enter into a life of worship themselves.

experiencing **worship**

May the church of God rise up and praise Him for the many things He has done and is doing! God wants to do so much more in our churches and in our lives. Until we begin to offer up true praise from the heart, I fear our churches will continue to stagnate and accomplish little for the Lord. It must begin somewhere. Will you be the one to step out and give Him praise?

Exercise for Week 3 - In your own words, with what you know about praise and worship, create a phrase that is your expression of what you feel for the Lord. Add it to what you have already been expressing. Remember that voicing this praise needs to be done daily. Continue to come to your weekly worship service with the attitude of giving. Do not look to gain from the service, only to give. Offer up praise in your church this week that is genuine and real. See if it makes a difference in your worship experience.

Write down what you experienced after week 3. Plan to share this with those in your group.

____

____

____

____

____

____

Continue in your daily devotional through the week. Share with someone close to you your heart for praising the Lord. Also, ask a friend or two what they feel praise is. You may be surprised with the many different answers you will find.

DAILY DEVOTIONS

WEEK 3

experiencing **worship**

DAY 1

"...the twenty-four elders fall down before him who sits on the throne, and worship him who lives for ever and ever. They lay their crowns before the throne and say: "You are worthy, our Lord and God, to receive glory and honor and power, for you created all things, and by your will they were created and have their being." Revelation 4:10-11 (NIV)

Imagine meeting God face to face. What do you think it will be like? I can't wait to see Jesus and ask Him all the unanswered questions that I have. I long to see God the Father to thank Him for sending His Son to die for me. What will it be like? We all have our visions of what that day will hold. I'm sure all the scenarios I've conjured up in my mind will be nothing compared to the reality of God and heaven. The truth is, I will probably be overwhelmed before the God of heaven. I imagine I will be on my face before Him.

The twenty-four elders described in Revelation are already in heaven. They have seen God, and yet they still fall down before Him. I pray that God will move me to a new respect of who He is and show me where my place is in worship. I tend to come before Him boldly, even arrogantly, when I should come before Him in humility and reverence because of who He is. Thank you, Lord, for helping me be more like you — with patience.

DAY 2

"The Lord says: 'These people come near to me with their mouth and honor me with their lips, but their hearts are far from me. Their worship of me is made up only of rules taught by men.'" Isaiah 29:13 (NIV)

I love Matt Redman's song, "The Heart of Worship." It has a truth that we all need to remember and return to.

> *"When the music fades and all is swept away and I simply come, longing just to bring something that's of worth, that will bless your heart, I'll give you more than a song, for a song in itself is not what you have required. You search much deeper within...* ***You're looking into my heart.*** *I'm coming back to the heart of worship, and it's all about You, all about You, Jesus."*[7]

This song pinpoints a simple truth about what worship should be. The Pharisees had their man-made rules for worship, which displeased God. In fact, men for years have put their traditions of worship and have squelched true worship. We often know what to say and do on the outside, but our hearts are far behind. God, however, desires our hearts to be involved in worship. He knows what we are feeling and thinking, yet we often act like we can " fool" Him with our actions. When we come to Him with a clean heart that is pure and we worship Him in spirit and truth, we will begin to become worshipers who worship from the heart and not just the head.

experiencing **worship**

DAY 3

"I will praise you as long as I live, and in your name I will lift up my hands." Psalm 63:4 (NIV)

Have you ever found yourself singing a song without realizing what you were singing? I am notorious for that. I sing songs all the time with little thought of the text or meaning. I used to always get the words wrong to many old songs. I never stopped to think about what the words meant; I just sang words like they sounded to me whether they made sense or not. This habit is still with me today.

In singing worship music, this is a dangerous habit. Consider, for example, singing, *"I will praise You as long as I live."* When I come to a song that has text like this psalm, I have to stop and ask myself, "Will I really do this? Can I say that I will praise the Lord as long as I live?" If I sing it, I should be willing to do it. After all, worship is my gift to God. If I say I am going to do something, I need to be willing to follow it through.

We need to be careful of what we say and of what we sing. There are some heavy texts to many hymns and choruses that we sing each week. I wonder if God is pleased when we sing empty words with no intent to follow through. If it is from the heart, we will sing it and do it. I hope that I will always be able to say that I will praise Him as long as I live. Can you?

"I will praise you, O LORD, among the nations; I will sing of you among the peoples." Psalm 108:3

For years I have been frustrated with churches that shy away from true worship on Sundays. It seems that we have become so concerned about not offending visitors that true worship has become a thing of the past. Besides, our purpose on earth is to win people to Christ right? "Maybe true worship will scare them off," we worry.

Nothing could be further from the truth. Sundays are about worship and teaching; they are for the believer. When Paul witnessed to people, He let them have it with the truth. He held nothing back. In love, through His bold, unique style of teaching, he shared the message of salvation.

Sadly, many churches today have lost their power. We no longer feel that God's word is sufficient to save and convict people of sin. When we sugar coat things on Sundays to prevent offending a visitor, we merely send them away with a small taste of decent music and a well-crafted but watered-down message. What they really need to experience is the word of God preached at full potency and genuine worship from God's children. Then they might say, "WOW, I want that!"

I challenge you to step back and take a hard look at your church. Are you praising Him among the nations or keeping Him from the lost?

DAY 5

"Immediately he received his sight and followed Jesus, praising God. When all the people saw it, they also praised God." Luke 18:43

How thankful are we? When we receive things that we know are from God, do we stop to thank Him and praise Him?

God has been doing some incredible things in my life lately. I know that each of them has come from Him. He continually blesses me. Why? I don't know. I do know that I will always be grateful to Him for it. When you are blessed, is your natural response, "Praise you, Lord!?" What do you think when good things happen to you? Is credit given where credit is due? I hope so.

The blind man in Luke 18 could have very well run off to his family and left Jesus behind. We see that after Jesus healed the ten lepers, only one returned to say thank you.

What was the outcome of this man's taking the time to praise for what Jesus had done? Others saw the miracle and in turn praised God. Praise is contagious.

When God is working, it shouldn't matter whom He is healing or blessing. What matters is that He is worthy of praise because He is God. I pray that we will all develop lives that give praise to God when we see Him working. Even when it's hard to see sometimes, He is still worthy of it. Give Him praise today.

NOTES

experiencing **worship**

WEEK 4

CORPORATE AND PERSONAL WORSHIP

Many of us think worship can only take place in the church. Some believe that God lives in a church building. Many believers go to a church building to pray, as if God will only hear them in "sanctuary." It is essential to understand that God is not confined to a building. He is everywhere – omnipresent. To confine God to a building limits His power and presence. The building is the place where the church body *comes together* to worship, but God can be worshiped anywhere. In becoming true worshipers, we need to know that we should worship Him wherever we are and we don't need to wait until Sundays.

CORPORATE WORSHIP

Some might say, "Why do we need to go to church if God can hear us wherever we are?" There is a good, biblical reason for our coming to church to worship.

Read Hebrews 10:24-25. What does it say about why we need to come to church to worship together?

____

____

PREPARATION FOR WORSHIP

When we do come together for corporate worship, we need to prepare for worship. If we have all the ingredients of worship but do not properly prepare ourselves for worship, it will be difficult to truly worship. We must spend time before the service to prepare our hearts and minds for worship. Just as a young woman might spend hours in front of the mirror getting ready for that first date, so must we prepare ourselves to meet with the Living God. Praying as you rise in the morning, singing along to a praise song on the way to church, and confessing sin in your life regularly will help your worship time to be much more meaningful and help you to be attuned to the Spirit of God.

List five ways that you can prepare yourself for worship:

1. ______________________________

2. ______________________________

3. ______________________________

4. ______________________________

5. ______________________________

Becoming a worshiper means that our minds must focus on the One we are worshiping. In our fast-paced world, it is a difficult thing to focus on anything for a long period of time, much less in a church service with all that could be going on. A boring sermon, a piano out of tune, or songs we don't like might all seem like valid excuses to us for not worshiping, but the Bible speaks differently on the subject.

Many of us are good about getting through the praise part of the service. We can enjoy singing upbeat songs about the good things God has done for us. The problem is that we often stop there, never really going beyond praise and entering into deeper worship. That's like driving 200 miles to see a football game and never entering the stadium to see and experience the game with all the sights and sounds of live football. Maybe you even stand outside of the stadium and cheer about how great your team is, but you don't really get to see the team at work because you don't go all the way in.

I believe that there are many churches – and even some ministers of music – who do not understand this. We are more concerned about putting together a good "song" service or "music" service that flows. The thought of truly worshiping is rarely addressed. And to be frank, I know there are ministers of music who do not understand worship themselves. I know it, because I was one of them. My personal life was not reflective of worship and, therefore, I had no concept of what it really meant to worship or to lead worship. I see other music ministers like this all the time.

I do not say this to be critical, but only as a confession and an observation with the hope of helping others become the worship leaders that Christ would have them to be. For many years I was that kind of a music minister, desiring to be a "worship leader," but not knowing how. It wasn't until I began reading and experimenting with worship that I began understanding what it meant to be a worshiper. I still have a long, long way to go before I am the worshiper God wants me to be, but He has revealed many things to me through scripture and other people, some of which I am sharing with you in this book.

PERSONAL WORSHIP

Read Psalm 34:1

____

____

Does it say *some* of the time? Or if the *conditions* are right?

____

What would it be like if you chose to show your love for your spouse, your children, your friends, or parents only once a week? Would these people feel that you truly loved them? Would they know their worth? I doubt it. The same principle applies to our relationship with the Lord. Becoming a true worshiper means that you worship regularly. In fact, there is none more worthy of our constant worship from day to day. ***Becoming a worshiper is a lifestyle — not a once-a-week activity.***

Relying on one visit to church each week to meet your spiritual needs won't get you very far in your spiritual growth. Worshiping once a week isn't enough to become the worshiper that God would have you be. Why would you choose to do something so valuable only once a week when you can do it every day?

Again, who was said to be a man after God's own heart?

____

Read the following scriptures and summarize the type of man David was:

Psalm 9:2 ____________________________

18:46 ____________________________

18:49 ____________________________

21:13 ____________________________

22:22 ____________________________

26:7 ____________________________

30:4 ____________________________

33:1 ____________________________

These are but a few of the scriptures of David's praise to the Lord. We can voice these ourselves as we give our praise to Him.

What can we learn from David the *"worshiper"*?

First, he worshiped in spite of his feelings. He worshiped because of his love for the Lord. He worshiped because he knew it was what God desired from him. He worshiped despite the sin in his life. He worshiped the holiness of God with a godly fear. He also worshiped all the time.

experiencing **worship**

Read what the psalmist says in Psalm 96:2-9. What does verse 9 say to us?

____

____

____

In our worship we must be like David and not hold anything back. Do you believe God is pleased with half-hearted singing or with only part of our attention? Is He pleased when we withhold part of our tithe or other resources? Do you believe that just showing up in church and filling a pew is pleasing to God?

When we come to understand God's holiness, we realize that it is an awe-inspiring thing — especially when we compare it to our unholiness. It is something to truly fear. We must realize how unholy we are when we come before the Lord in worship. We ought to fear – knowing that God could, if He wanted to, take our very lives and cast them into hell. It is only by His grace that He chooses not to even though we deserve it. David understood this very well.

What does Hebrews 12:28-29 say in regard to this?

____

____

____

This example can be compared to fire fighters. Even though fire fighters have the protection of fire-proof suits and other equipment, they still fear the fire because they understand what it can do; they know its power. They have a sense of respect for it. Similarly, we as believers might be fully "protected" with our salvation, yet we have reverence for the Lord because we know His power.

What happened when people of the Bible stood before the Lord? How did they respond to His holiness? Summarize the responses in the following passages:

Exodus 20:18-20 ________________________________

____

____

Job 42:5-6 ________________________________

____

____

Judges 13:21-22 ________________________________

____

Haggai 1:12 ________________________________

How we worship is important, but it's who we worship that is most important.

I want to share a little about what I mean by this statement. Throughout the years, different denominations have disagreed on how we are to worship. Some people are more expressive outwardly than others. I believe that we all worship according to how God has created us. Though we are in His image, God has made us each of us unique, and through that uniqueness we come to Him with our worship.

Some people I know love the Lord with all their heart, soul, and mind, and some of these raise their hands in worship and some don't. On the other hand, I also know people who raise their hands in worship continually and yet their lives have no reflection of Christ. Clearly, exterior worship styles do not matter.

What does matter to God — what makes your worship acceptable to Him — is worshiping sincerely from your heart in your genuine way. Just as God has created each of us to do a specific ministry here on earth, a personal life mission that is unique to us, so He has created us to worship Him. We worship Him in a manner that is acceptable to Him and comes uniquely from ourselves — not mimicking someone else's expressions or style of worship.

Read Psalm 24:3-4. What does it say about our preparation?

MY STORY

I grew up in a conservative Baptist church where my father was the pastor. We were very involved in our church and all of its programs, from music to outreach. Our church reached hundreds of people through the years through my parents' ministry there. It was a great church where my parents served faithfully.

Growing up, though, I never knew what worship was. To me it was coming to church and holding out until the end so I could go home and go to the beach with my friends. Worship to me was going to church. That is what we called it — a "worship service." I don't recall seeing many outward expressions of worship in our church. We were considered a conservative church in theology and worship style. I had visited other denominations growing up that had more visible worship styles. Yet even then, it didn't mean anything to me, because I did not know Christ personally at that time.

It wasn't until I accepted Christ as my Savior that I desired to express to Him my gratefulness for what He had done for me. I wanted to dance and sing as an expression of thankfulness. I wept as the burden of sin was lifted from my life. I finally had it in me to *worship* then because I knew Christ as my Savior and Lord.

However, I didn't have anyone who helped me further my understanding of what I was doing at the time. Once the emotional part of my salvation experience wore off, so did my worship. I retreated back to my life of *enduring* church. I didn't realize that worship was giving praise to the Lord through singing and through actively listening to His word being preached. I didn't understand that it didn't matter what I felt like; I needed to give myself to the Lord, always thanking Him for what He has done in my life and for who He is. I thought that receiving a *feeling* was what you were supposed to get out of worship — it was, in my mind, the *goal* of worship. I didn't know that emotion was only a by-product of true worship.

Years went by, too many I am ashamed to say, before I really began to discover and seek out this thing called worship. I served in several churches where I went through the motions of a worship service, which was really a music service, not knowing what I was doing.

Eventually, I began to read books by men like John McArthur, Lamar Boschman, Tom Kraeuter, and Jack Hayford, who have a far better understanding of worship than I do. Listening to the music of Dennis Jernigan, Paul Baloche, Darlene Zschech, and Bob Fitts, I began to discover not only what worship was, but what it is to be a worshiper. I became hungry to learn more, and through my learning, my worship life finally became real and meaningful. It was like an addiction of the best kind. I couldn't get enough of it!

experiencing **worship**

As I began to uncover the truth about worship, I realized that it was something that we are to do on a daily basis and not just Sunday mornings. What a revelation it was for me! I could actually worship in my car driving to work or in the shower as I was getting ready. It didn't matter where or what I was doing. I could worship my Creator and Lord anywhere. What a life-changing revelation! I discovered that because of my daily personal worship, my corporate worship was even more meaningful. As a worship pastor, what I did in my personal time flowed over to the congregational time. ***Then I became a real worship leader and not just a song leader.***

At that point in my journey, I felt I had a small understanding of worship and I wanted to help others know more in order to become the worshipers that God would have them be. I wanted others to truly *experience worship.* My life's mission became to help others better understand biblical worship and begin to become worshipers who are pleasing to God and who worship Him in spirit and truth.

Today I better understand worship and what it means to be a worshiper. I don't know all there is about it, and I still desire to be a more effective worship pastor every day. I want to help others discover what I have learned. I hope to help young Christians know what it is to be a worshiper early on in their walk with the Lord. I don't want them to wait 20 years before they figure out what they were created for.

corporate and personal worship

Exercise for Week 4 - During your daily worship times, express your own words of praise and worship for the Lord. Begin to use scripture. Remember that this needs to be done daily. Continue to attend a weekly worship service with the attitude of giving. Do not look to gain from the service, only to give.

Write down what you experienced after week 4. Plan to share this with those in your group.

____

____

____

____

Continue in your daily devotional. Turn your quiet times into times of worship as you study God's word and as He reveals to you His desires for you.

experiencing **worship**

DAILY DEVOTIONS

WEEK 4

experiencing **worship**

DAY 1

"Worship the LORD in the splendor of his holiness; tremble before him, all the earth." Psalm 96:9 (NIV)

As a young teenager, I would find myself at the beach regularly. You see, I grew up in Hawaii where I learned to surf at an early age. It was my life for many years. Because I was introduced to the ocean at an early age, I rarely stopped to examine its true power. I was a surfer –invincible! It wasn't until I had a near-death experience that I began to respect the mighty power of the ocean and to acknowledge my mortality.

How similar this is to many Christians in the arena of worship! We come to church week after week with little regard for God's power and holiness. We sit through the service with everything on our minds except God and His might. We go through the motions of church and leave no different from when we arrived.

If we knew the true power of God and understood His holiness, we would tremble with fear as we come before Him in worship. We would find ourselves on our knees and faces, unworthy of standing before Him. Instead, we come before Him boldly and arrogantly as if to say, "Lord this is our time and this is what we want." Think about who He is! Come before Him with reverence. He is holy — set apart by His immense power and purity.

DAY 2

"*Lift up your hands in the sanctuary and praise the LORD.*"
Psalm 134:2 (NIV)

Many expressions of worship are mentioned in the Bible. Aside from the use of tongues, this could be the next in line for controversy in the church. Many churches argue that the lifting up of our hands is really just an attention-seeking distraction in worship. "It's not proper etiquette to raise your hands in worship," many would say. "It only draws attention to yourself," others would add. "Besides, it's not very reverent."

However, raising hands is mentioned several times in the Bible. To say it's not a true expression of worship is only a lack of understanding. What does raising our hands really say? It wasn't meant to draw attention to us; it's an act of humility toward God. Like bowing down, lifting up our hands to God exalts His greatness. It is a physical way of saying, "I am like a child in your presence. You are my Abba, my spiritual Father, my Daddy. I honor You."

It can also be a celebration of the Lord. Watch any sporting event and see what the players and fans do when they score a goal or points. Up go the hands in celebration — clapping, stretching overhead, doing the wave! Wouldn't you say that Christians have more to celebrate that anyone on earth? Then why do we hide it? Why do we feel like we have to keep it inside?

experiencing **worship**

DAY 3

"*Therefore I tell you, whatever you ask for in prayer, believe that you have received it, and it will be yours.*" Mark 11:24 (NIV)

Behind every great revival in history there has been prayer. Behind every move of God there has been prayer. James 5:16-18 tells us that "the prayer of a righteous man is powerful and effective. Elijah was a man just like us. He prayed earnestly that it would not rain, and it did not rain on the land for three and a half years. Again he prayed, and the heavens gave rain, and the earth produced its crops."

Today we still have that power. The power of prayer has not diminished one bit. Why is it, then, that God is not moving across our country the way we would like? Why is sin so prevalent in all we do? Often, it is because we fail to pray. We fail to ask God to be God in our homes and country. Our worship services fail to offer times of lengthy prayer. We are more concerned about people "getting the message," when what they need to learn to do is pray. Nothing can replace time spent on our knees, and yet we refuse to do it.

This week, as part of your worship, spend twice the time you normally do in prayer. See if it affects your week in a real, tangible way. God longs for us to merely ask.

DAY 4

"*I love the LORD, for he heard my voice; he heard my cry for mercy.*" Psalm 116:1 (NIV)

It seems odd to me that this phrase is rarely used in the Bible. There are not many verses that say, "I love you, Lord." It seems strange, because Deuteronomy 6:5 says, "Love the LORD your God with all your heart and with all your soul and with all your strength." We find this saying mentioned several times in the Bible. Why is it, then, that the writers of scripture so rarely tell God they love Him? Why is the Bible not filled with God's people proclaiming their love to the Lord?

Oddly enough, they do. Following many verses that command us to love the Lord, there is a tag that says, "to walk in His way." How do we love the Lord? Is it through our mouths or through our *actions*? I don't believe God is pleased when we *say* we love Him, but our actions contradict our words.

In John 21, when Jesus asked Peter three times, "Do you love me?" Peter responded, "yes" each time. Jesus followed with, "then feed my sheep." Jesus' teaching shows that true love is shown in action. Love is a verb. In marriage, true love is shown by what we do and not only by what we say. John 15:13 (NIV) says, "*Greater love has no one than this, that he lay down his life for his friends.*" It's more than words; it's action. As we grow as worshipers, may we show our love to God by being obedient to Him through the things we do and not only by what we say.

DAY 5

"*Love the LORD your God with all your heart and with all your soul and with all your strength.*" Deuteronomy 6:5 (NIV)

What is the greatest form of worship? To do these very things – to love the Lord with our heart, strength, and soul. Then we will develop lives of true worship of the Father. Worship isn't only what we do on Sundays. It's more than raising a song or our hands to the Lord. ***A life of true worship consists of giving to God everything we are.***

If He asks us to give, we need to give. If He asks us to bow on our faces before Him, we need to do it. The Bible is our life's manual. How we choose to respond to its direction will determine who we will be in Christ.

I pray that each of us will seek, love, pray, and praise God more each day of our lives. I pray we will be obedient to all He asks of us. We can never get too much of God. May He say of all of us one day, "You were people after my own heart."

NOTES

WEEK 5

A TRUE WORSHIPER

A TRUE WORSHIPER

Over the past several weeks, you have been discovering this thing called praise and worship. In fact, if you have been following the few bits of direction from the scripture, you have experienced worship.

Becoming a true worshiper involves taking on several characteristics, aside from just giving our praise to God in an outward manner. Because worship is a natural reaction to our salvation, our lives must reflect ***on a daily*** basis Christ and His will for our lives. We must be involved in outreach (calling others to become worshipers), giving of our time, talents, and resources, living lives that are holy and acceptable to God, following the commandments to love our neighbors as ourselves, and seeking to be all that God would have us be. Our lives must reflect Christ in all that we do. How can we give praise to God and hate our brother? Becoming a true worshiper is more than just what we do in our worship services — it is a lifestyle of evangelism, spiritual growth, worship and praise, discipleship, and giving. It is discovering who God made you to be, identifying your life's mission and calling, and pursuing it with all you are.

As we seek to become the worshipers who God would desire each of us to be, we must understand that our emotions should not keep us from worshiping. We do not worship only when it feels right. Worship is not always a euphoric experience. It can be and will be on some occasions, but in becoming a true worshiper, our feelings cannot be the *reason* we worship. Worshiping each day of our lives is what God created us for. He knew that we would have good days when it would be easy to worship Him and bad days when we would not feel like worshiping Him. Those who truly love Him will sacrifice self to worship the living God continually.

Read the following instances in the Bible and respond to what happened:

Job 1:13-22 ____

____

____

____

2 Samuel 12:18-20 ____

____

____

____

These men were true worshipers of God. They are characterized by their understanding that even in the lowest times in their lives, they knew where to turn. They weren't expecting to be comforted by the Lord but gave Him the worship that He deserved — despite how they felt.

How far toward this goal have you come in your own worship life?

____

____

____

____

experiencing **worship**

Even though the instinct to worship is born within every man, we still need to learn how to worship. Read Psalm 89:15. What does it say about how we are to worship?

____

____

____

____

Even though you might have read each passage in this study and know what it means to be a worshiper, you must still put these thing into practice to be a worshiper. No one begins writing or speaking at birth; they must learn to write and talk. The same applies to worship.

Let's look again at John 4:23 (NKJV) "*But an hour is coming, and now is, when the true worshipers shall worship the Father in spirit and truth; for such the Father seeks to be His worshipers.*"

What is it that the Father *seeks*? (Circle One)

Worship or Worshipers

What does it mean to "*worship in truth?*" Consider this: Do Muslims worship in truth? They do worship. In fact, they are very sincere and committed in their worship. They believe that they are worshiping the one true God. However, we know that they do not worship the God of the Bible. In order to understand the one true God, you have to know and understand the Bible. You must know this God through a personal relationship.

John 14:6 (NIV) says, *"Jesus answered, 'I am the way and the truth and the life. No one comes to the Father except through Me.'"* The expression *"to worship Him in truth"* refers to worship that is in keeping with the nature of God. It is worship that is love filled and love based. It is pure in its motive to please the One True God. But most importantly, it is worship that recognizes that the only way for us to enter God's presence is through Christ. That is the truth of the Bible.

What is it to *"worship the Father in spirit?"* It is simply our spirit in accord with the spirit of God. It is not a fleshly thing or merely vocalizing it. It must come from our innermost spirit to His Spirit. Many worship out of lip service and tradition and not truly in the spirit.

Look at Isaiah 29:13. What does it say?

____

____

____

____

It's easy to get caught up in the actions of worship and leave the Spirit behind. I believe that this scripture is saying that when we worship, we need to tune out the things of the world and tune into Him alone.

We need to focus on His Spirit. When we are truly worshiping the Lord, His Spirit will be in tune with our spirit. His Spirit will lead us in what to do. If we insist on worshiping in our own selves and beings, we will never experience true spirit worship. Remember this is the type of worshiper that God seeks.

THE OBEDIENCE FACTOR

What is the key to serving God? Is it taking the good things He has to offer, the things that we are comfortable with, and leaving the rest behind? Is it a spiritual buffet? In the same vein, what is the key to true worship? Is it taking the elements that we like (singing, clapping, dancing, etc.) and leaving the hard parts for someone else?

The Bible is very clear on how we are to live. God has given us His Ten Commandments. In the New Testament He elaborates on these further and even adds to the laws. Take, for example, "Thou shalt not murder." Jesus says if you hate your brother you have committed murder in your heart already. The same is said of adultery. We know the "laws." We know how we are supposed to live our lives – loving our neighbors as ourselves. Seems simple enough, right?

How does obedience factor into worship? We have seen that worship is not an option for the believer. God requires it of us. God tells us to worship and even gives us acceptable ways to do it. It is our job to be willing to obey.

I love the life of David. It's interesting to read through the Psalms and see the many various ways that David worshiped. How about us? What do we do during our worship times? How do we worship? What are we able to do and still be reverent before the Lord? What is God's desire in our worship?

The Psalms give us nine different expressions of worship. These expressions stem from David's desire to worship the Lord wholeheartedly – without reservation. Oddly enough, these expressions are not foreign to us, and yet we fail to practice them in our corporate worship for one reason or another. Listed below are the nine expressions of worship that we will focus on. They can be broken down in three physical expressions.

A. OUR SPOKEN VOICE

1. Speaking - Psalm 34:1 (NIV) says, *"I will extol the Lord at all times; his praise will always be on my lips."*
2. Shouting - Psalm 27:6 (NIV) says, *"Then my head will be exalted above the enemies who surround me; at his tabernacle will I sacrifice with shouts of joy; I will sing and make music to the Lord."*
3. Singing - Psalm 47:6 (NIV) says, *"Sing praises to God, sing praises to our King, sing praises."*

B. OUR POSTURE

1. Bowing - Psalm 95:6 (NIV) says, *"Come let us bow down in worship, let us kneel before the LORD our Maker."*
2. Standing - Psalm 119:120 (NIV) says, *"My flesh trembles in fear of you; I stand in awe of your laws."*
3. Dancing - Psalm 149:3 (NIV) says, *"Let them praise his name with dancing and make music to him with tambourine and harp."*

C. OUR HANDS

1. Playing Instruments - Psalm 33:2-3 (NIV) says, *"Praise the Lord with the harp; make music to him on the ten-stringed lyre. Sing to him a new song; play skillfully, and shout for joy."*
2. Clapping - Psalm 47:1 (NIV) says, *"Clap your hands, all you nations; shout to God with cries of joy."*
3. Raising of Hands - Psalm 63:4 (NIV) says, *"I will praise you as long as I live, and in your name I will lift up my hands."*

None of these expressions is foreign to us, are they? They may be foreign to our worship experiences, but they are not to our culture. When there is a wedding and the bridal march begins, what do we do without thinking twice? We stand in honor of the bride and groom on this special day in their lives. When a man asks a woman to marry him, he gets on his knee to propose to her. Why? Because he wants to show her that he honors her. Dancing is no stranger to our culture. We clap for everything that pleases us. Those who can will play their instruments for hour on hour even with no audience. When someone gives us a gift, we immediately speak our thanks. Have you ever been to a ball game where the parents of the players were present? If so, you've experienced shouting at its best. Even those who claim they "can't sing" do sing – in cars, showers, and sometimes on stage. We are a musical people. And whenever a player scores a basket or touchdown, our hands fly up in the air. It is a natural response to an amazing task performed.

Why share all this? We know it, right? And yet, though we might do these things in other areas of our lives, many of us fail to exercise these in public worship. They seem unnatural to us, uncomfortable even. Yet David used these expressions because he wanted to worship God with his entire being. He had a great heart to worship the Lord with everything he had. He held nothing back in his worship. If only we were willing to honor God as radically as we honor wives, sports heroes, and our favorite musicians! If only we took such great delight in pleasing the Lord through God's creation – our bodies and souls!

What else can we learn from David? He not only practiced these expressions regularly, he didn't care one bit what others thought about it. Even his wife thought he was crazy, and yet God thought enough of his worship to call him "a man after His own heart." Who is our audience? Who are we trying to please in worship? It better be God. Is He pleased with your worship? I hope He is with mine.

I challenge you to seek the Lord in these expressions. Ask Him what He would have you do in your times of worship. Is your heart moved to dance before the Lord, yet you choose to sit? Does the Spirit move you to get on your face before the Lord, yet you remain standing because you are afraid of what the person next to you will say? Remember, worship is not about you. It's not about your neighbor. It's about letting the Lord lead you to worship Him in a manner that He desires and you need. What benefit could we possibly gain from kneeling before the Lord? How about humility? What could be gained from shouting to the Lord? How about boldness to speak His name in public? What could we learn from lifting our hands to the Lord? How about submission to Him? James 4:6 (NIV) tells us, *"But he gives us more grace. That is why the scripture says: 'God opposes the proud but gives grace to the humble.'"*

Let us grow in our worship to the Lord. Let us allow His Spirit to move in us as we worship. Let God direct your actions and responses. What we receive is a heart of humility, grace, and reverence before God. He is the One who saved us from sin and called us to be His children forever. Be obedient to His leading in your worship. If He leads you to express yourself in one of the nine ways mentioned in the Psalms, try it! Until we are totally obedient to the Lord in our worship and in our lives, we will never know all He has for us.

If you feel that you are never going to be a "great" worshiper and this is just too much to take in, if you feel that there is no way to understand all this stuff and that maybe this kind of worship is only for certain people, don't fret. Worship is not meant to be a frustrating, unattainable thing. It is simple and for the simple. Worship should be a relaxing, meaningful time with your Creator and King. It is not a difficult thing to It is not a difficult thing to *"be still and know that He is God."* Rest in Him as you worship.

Take several minutes to answer the questions below. You will find them familiar, as you answered them during the first week of this study. My hope is that your answers will be different now, that you will come away with a deeper understanding of worship, and that you will be a true worshiper who worships Him in spirit and truth.

experiencing **worship**

In your own words, give your definition of worship.

____

____

____

What is the place of worship in a Christian's life as you understand it?

____

____

____

____

What is the place of worship in your life now?

____

____

Do you feel that you are now a worshiper?

Yes　　No　　I am starting to be one　　Still not sure

As with any teaching on how we are to live our lives, I must say that your decision to respond to God in worship is between you and Him. We are all responsible to obey His commands, share Him with others, and be faithful to Him throughout our lives. It's up to you to seek these things and find out what He would have you do in everything.

I challenge you to grow in your relationship with the Father. He wants us to experience all that He has for us--all that He created us to be. Our lives are not designed to merely exist; we were created for so much more. Be a mentor to someone as they seek to become a worshiper of our Lord.

ONE LAST THOUGHT

I challenge you to grow in your relationship with the Father. He wants us to experience all that He has for us – all that He created us to be. Our lives are not designed to merely exist; we were created for so much more. Be a mentor to others as they seek to become worshipers of our Lord. I challenge you to continue to pursue a life that is ***Experiencing Worship*** every day.

ORDERING INFORMATION

To order this study for your worship team, choir, leadership, or small groups, visit our site at www.ExperiencingWorship.com

FOR MORE RESOURCES ON WORSHIP VISIT

www.ExperiencingWorship.com

---

[1] Boschman, Lamar, A Heart of Worship: Experience a Rebirth of Worship, Orlando, Fla.: Creation House, 1994, p.58.

[2] Ibid., p.60.

[3] Ibid., p.22.

[4] Ibid., p.61.

[5] Webster's Revised Unabridged Dictionary, Plainfield, N. J.: MICRA, 1998.

[6] Webster's Revised Unabridged Dictionary, Plainfield, N. J.: MICRA, 1998.

[7] Redmon, Matt, "A Heart of Worship," EMI Christian Music Group, 1999.